spot

OCEAN ANIMALS

JELLYFISH

by Mari Schuh

AMICUS | AMICUS INK

bell

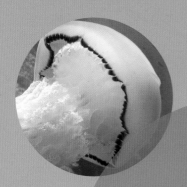

tentacles

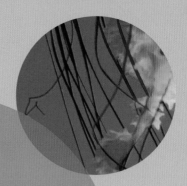

Look for these
words and pictures
as you read.

arms

mouth

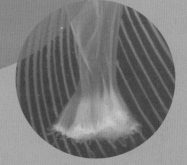

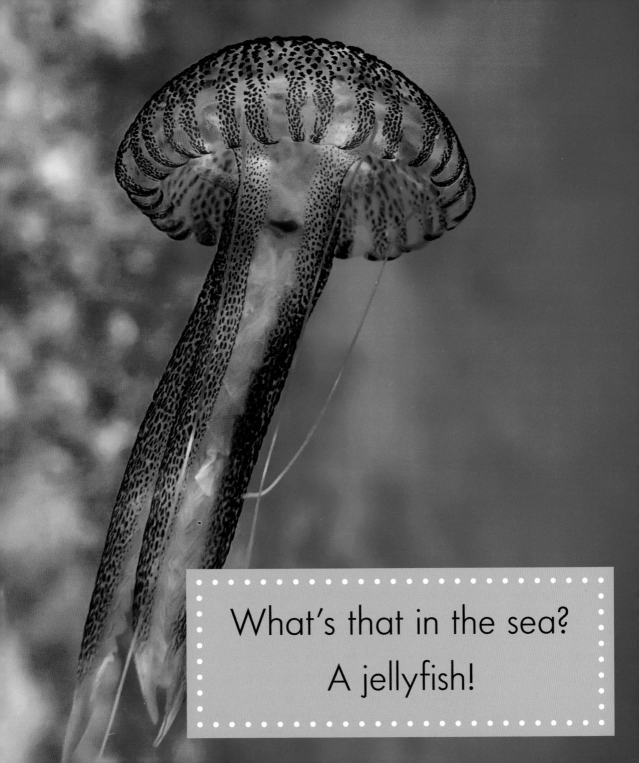

What's that in the sea?
A jellyfish!

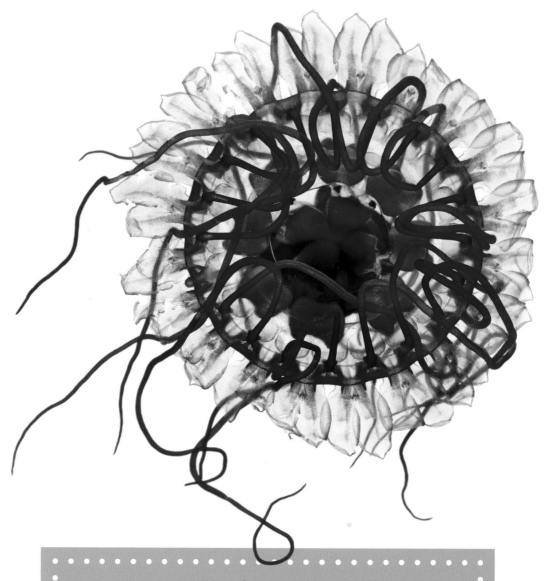

A jellyfish is soft.
It does not have bones.

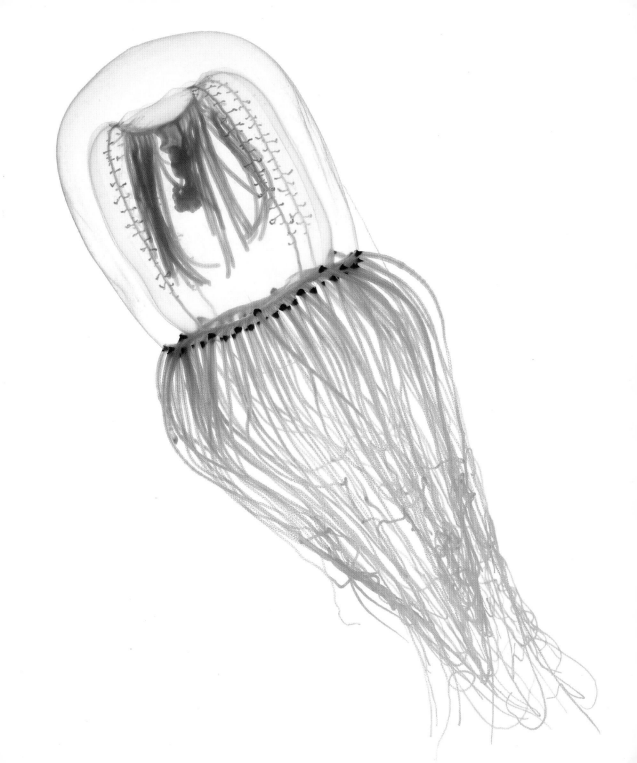

Look at the bell.
It is the body.
It is soft and squishy.

bell

tentacles

Look at the tentacles.
They feel for prey.
They sting, too.

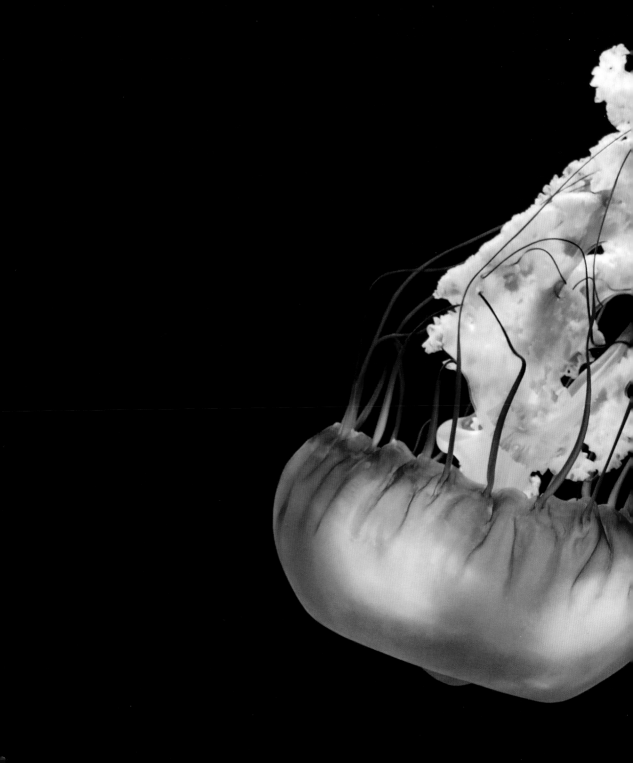

arms

Look at the arms.
They are thick.
They grab prey.

Look at the mouth.
It eats prey whole.
It also gets rid of waste.

mouth

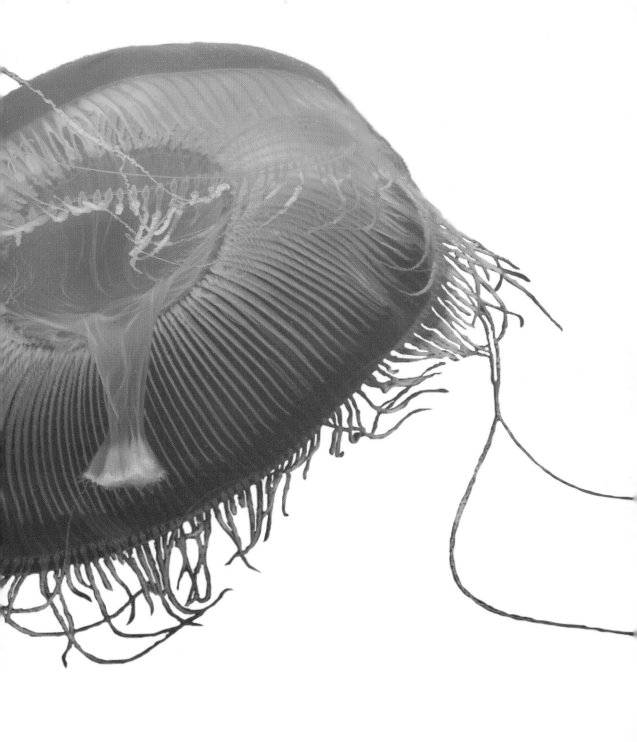

Look at it float!

Waves carry it away.

Bye, bye!

Look at the bell.
It is the body.
It is soft and squishy.

bell

tentacles

Look at the tentacles.
They feel for prey.
They sting, too.

bell

tentacles

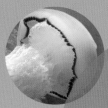

Did you find?

arms

mouth

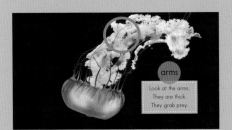

arms

Look at the arms.
They are thick.
They grab prey.

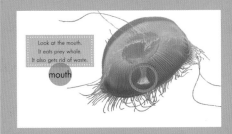

Look at the mouth.
It eats prey whole.
It also gets rid of waste.

mouth

Spot is published by Amicus and Amicus Ink
P.O. Box 1329, Mankato, MN 56002
www.amicuspublishing.us

Library of Congress Cataloging-in-Publication Data
Names: Schuh, Mari C., 1975- author.
Title: Jellyfish / by Mari Schuh.
Description: Mankato, Minnesota : Spot/Amicus, [2019] |
   Series: Ocean animals | Audience: K to grade 3.
Identifiers: LCCN 2017020471 (print) | LCCN 2017027504
   (ebook) | ISBN 9781681514628 (eBook) | ISBN
   9781681513805 (library binding) | ISBN 9781681523002
   (paperback)
Subjects: LCSH: Jellyfishes--Juvenile literature.
Classification: LCC QL377.S4 (ebook) |
   LCC QL377.S4 S382 2019 (print) | DDC 593.5/3--dc23
LC record available at https://lccn.loc.gov/2017020471

Printed in China

HC 10 9 8 7 6 5 4 3 2 1
PB 10 9 8 7 6 5 4 3 2 1

To Natalie –MS

Rebecca Glaser, editor
Deb Miner, series designer
Ciara Beitlich, book designer
Holly Young, photo researcher

Photos by Alamy Stock Photo/Goran
Šafarek, 14–15; Getty Images, cover,
16; iStock, 3; National Geographic
Creative/David Liittschwager, 4, 5;
Shutterstock, 1, 6–7, 8–9, 10–11, 12–13

JELLYFISH